HAMSTERS

by Liza Jacobs

BLACKBIRCH®
PRESS

THOMSON
GALE

San Diego • Detroit • New York • San Francisco • Cleveland • New Haven, Conn. • Waterville, Maine • London • Munich

For more information, contact
The Gale Group, Inc.
27500 Drake Rd.
Farmington Hills, MI 48331-3535
Or you can visit our Internet site at http://www.gale.com

Photographs © 1995 by Chang Yi-Wen

Cover Photograph © Corbis

© 1995 by Chin-Chin Publications Ltd.

No. 274-1, Sec.1 Ho-Ping E. Rd., Taipei, Taiwan, R.O.C.
Tel: 886-2-2363-3486 Fax: 886-2-2363-6081

LIBRARY OF CONGRESS CATALOGING-IN-PUBLICATION DATA

Jacobs, Liza.
  Hamsters / by Liza Jacobs.
    p. cm. -- (Wild wild world)
  Summary: Describes the physical characteristics and habits of hamsters
and how to care for them as pets.
  Includes bibliographical references.
    ISBN 1-41030-038-2 (hardback : alk. paper)
    1. Hamsters as pets--Juvenile literature. 2. Hamsters--Juvenile
literature. [1. Hamsters. 2. Pets.] I. Title. II. Series.

SF459.H3 J33 2003
636.9'356--dc21
                                                              2002152044

Printed in Taiwan
10 9 8 7 6 5 4 3 2 1

Table of Contents

About Hamsters

A hamster is a type of mammal called a rodent.

All rodents have two pairs of large, sharp front teeth called incisors (see above).

These teeth are made for gnawing. They look a little like sharp chisels.

Rodents also have smaller cheek teeth for chewing.

There are many kinds of hamsters in the wild. They live in dry places such as deserts.

People also keep hamsters as pets.

A pet hamster needs a cage it cannot chew through. It needs soft materials for the floor and bed. (The box on the left is just for carrying a hamster home from the pet store.)

It also needs places to play and exercise.

These are some things you may put inside a hamster cage.

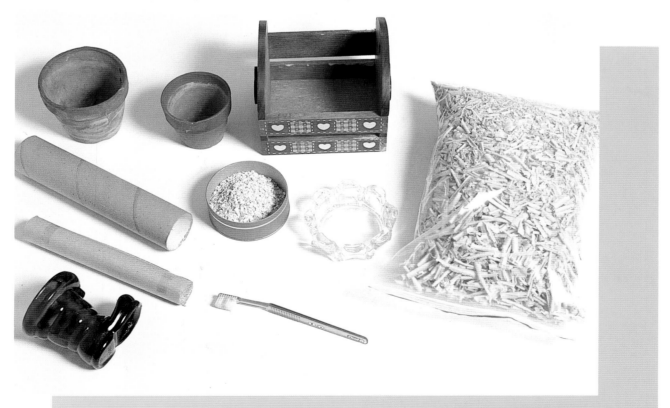

Hamster Bodies

Hamsters are small animals. They are about 3 to 7 inches long and weigh about 4 ounces.

They have soft fur that keeps them warm.

There are many different colors of fur, too—blond, yellow, white, brown, gray, and mixed colors.

Hamster eyesight is not very good.

Hamsters walk on all fours, but they often stand up straight on their back legs.

They usually do this to get a better look at something.

Grooming

Hamsters spend a lot
of time cleaning, or
grooming, themselves.

They wash themselves
with their tongue and paws.

Hamsters use their teeth to
nibble tangles out of their fur.

Five claws on the back paws
are used like combs.

Longhaired pet hamsters need to be brushed so their fur doesn't get tangled.

Food

After a good grooming, a hamster is ready to eat.

Hamsters eat all kinds of food. In the wild, they like to eat vegetables, insects, seeds, and grains.

Pet hamsters eat many things, including greens, carrots, corn, egg, cheese, and even meat.

All hamsters need plenty of water.

Hamsters do not eat all of their food right away.

Instead, they hide some of it in storage spots.

They carry off the food by filling large pouches in their cheeks.

Pet hamsters find places in their cage to store food.

In the wild, a hamster stores food in its home, or burrow.
A hamster uses its sharp front claws to dig its burrow.

Resting and Playing

Hamsters are nocturnal.

That means they sleep during the day and are active at night.

Hamsters build nests for sleeping.

They will chew through anything they can. Never give them materials such as plastic. This could make a pet hamster sick.

Once a hamster makes its cozy nest, it settles in to sleep.

Some like to dive underneath the nest. Others curl up in a warm ball.

A baby hamster is called a pup.

Pups grow inside a female hamster for about 16 days.

When a female gives birth, it has many babies at once.

They often have 8 to 10 pups. But a hamster can give birth to up to 24 little ones!

Newborn pups are tiny. They are only about an inch long.

They are born without fur. Their skin is pink and wrinkled.

Hamster pups huddle up together to keep warm.

Newborn hamsters are also deaf and blind. But a baby pup can smell its mother. It knows how to find its mother's milk.

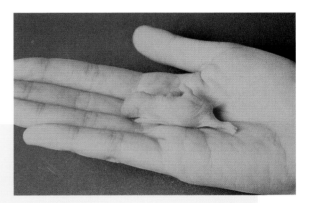

Newborn Life

After 3 or 4 days, the babies begin to grow a few hairs on their bodies.

They have little nubs that will become their ears.

A mother hamster keeps the nest safe and cozy for her pups.

She nurses her baby hamsters for 3 weeks. This helps them grow.

The mother hamster carries her babies in her mouth.

She can hold several babies in her cheek pouches at once.

This way, she can move them quickly to safety if she needs to.

A hamster mother carries her pup in her mouth.

Growing Up

When the pups are about 1 week old, they begin to eat solid food.

They have a thin coat of fur at about 10 days old.

Babies now start to explore a bit farther away from their mother.

The pups have grown to about 2 inches long.

In a few more days, they can see and hear.

After about 2 weeks, a baby hamster has a soft, furry coat.

Playing and Cuddling

After just 5 weeks, a pup is ready to live on its own.

By 4 months, it is full grown.

Young hamsters spend a lot of time together.

They play together and sleep cuddled up in groups.

When a hamster sleeps, it folds its ears flat. At most all other times, a hamster's ears stand upright.

Wonderful Pets

If a pet hamster is not sleeping or nibbling on something, it is usually running around.

This is also how hamsters behave in the wild.

Hamsters like to keep moving. Pet hamsters love to play in tunnels and run on exercise wheels.

Hamsters are clean, gentle, quiet animals.

They make wonderful pets!

For More Information

Evans, Mark. *Hamster* (ASPCA Pet Care Guide). New York: DK Publishing, 2001.

Holub, Joan. *Why Do Rabbits Hop? And Other Questions About Rabbits, Guinea Pigs, Hamsters, and Gerbils.* New York: Puffin, 2003.

Murray, Julie. *Hamsters*. Edina, MN: Abdo & Daughters, 2002.

Rockwell, Anne F. *My Pet Hamster* (Let's-Read-and-Find-Out Science). New York: HarperCollins, 2002.

Glossary

burrow a hamster's home in the wild

nocturnal asleep during the day and active at night

pup a baby hamster